Date: 5/8/17

Uu

Bela Davis

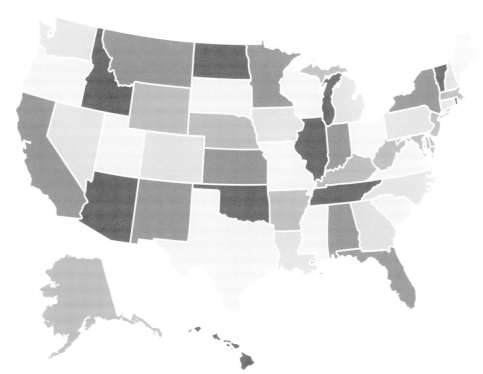

Abdo
THE ALPHABET
Kids

abdopublishing.com

Published by Abdo Kids, a division of ABDO, PO Box 398166, Minneapolis, Minnesota 55439.
Copyright © 2017 by Abdo Consulting Group, Inc. International copyrights reserved in all countries.
No part of this book may be reproduced in any form without written permission from the publisher.

Printed in the United States of America, North Mankato, Minnesota.

102016

012017

THIS BOOK CONTAINS
RECYCLED MATERIALS

Photo Credits: iStock, NASA, Shutterstock, ©Daniel M. Silva p.9, ©Aspen Photo p.23/Shutterstock.com

Production Contributors: Teddy Borth, Jennie Forsberg, Grace Hansen

Design Contributors: Christina Doffing, Candice Keimig, Dorothy Toth

Publisher's Cataloging in Publication Data

Names: Davis, Bela, author.

Title: Uu / by Bela Davis.

Description: Minneapolis, Minnesota : Abdo Kids, 2017 | Series: The alphabet |
    Includes bibliographical references and index.

Identifiers: LCCN 2016943901 | ISBN 9781680808971 (lib. bdg.) |
    ISBN 9781680796070 (ebook) | ISBN 9781680796742 (Read-to-me ebook)

Subjects: LCSH: English language--Alphabet--Juvenile literature. | Alphabet
    books--Juvenile literature.

Classification: DDC 421/.1--dc23

LC record available at http://lccn.loc.gov/2016943901

Table of Contents

Uu

Usher dives **u**nder the water.

Uu

Summer h**u**gs her **u**ncle.

Uu

The **um**pire calls an o**u**t.

Uu

Dustin wears a **uniform**.

Uu

Urban waits **u**ntil it is his t**u**rn.

Uu

Uri r**u**ns **u**p a hill.

14

Uu

Uma is **upset**.

16

Uu

Judd **u**ses a bl**u**e pen.

Uu

What is **U**li holding?

(an **u**mbrella)

More **Uu** Words

ukulele

unicycle

unhappy

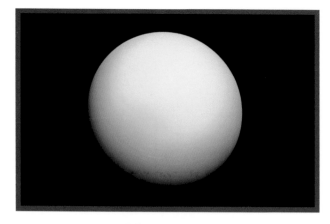

Uranus

Glossary

umpire
a person who watches a game to
enforce rules and make decisions.

uniform
matching clothing worn by children
attending a certain school.

upset
unhappy.

Index

abdokids.com

Use this code to log on to abdokids.com and access crafts, games, videos, and more!

Abdo Kids Code:
TUK8971